AF488450

# *for* Emerie,

whose spirit sustained her in sickness,
and to every child who will battle for their health;
may a steadfast spirit also sustain you.

*(proverbs 18:14)*

ISBN 979-8-218-56569-5
Copyright © 2024 Stand & Fight Foundation
All rights reserved.
Written by Stacie Schilling
Illustrated by Babi Wrobel
Book Design by Leigh Shaw // Illustration Online LLC

# Stand & Fight

## Overcoming the Giants in the Land

Written by
Stacie Schilling

Illustrated by
Babi Wrobel

Running! Laughing! Jumping! Playing!
What joy these activities bring!
Yet, I hardly had energy for a single thing.

Many friends came knocking at the door;
however, I felt lethargic while flopping on the floor.

Friends would call, "Come out to play!"
I would counter, "No, not today."

A flight of stairs I could hardly make;
how could I participate?

This condition was not shaking;
it was quite an undertaking.

My symptoms persisted; to the hospital, we bound.
I dressed in a threadbare gown.
Immediately, the doctors began to frown.

A look of conviction,
I scarcely heard them say,
"You will have to stay.
You have a rare condition.
We're not typically in this position."

I began to pale.
The heavy burden felt the size of a humpback whale.
The walls were caving in.
My emotions were in a tailspin.

I lay in bed, needing peace.
Over my head, I pulled the fleece.

Dad, peeking under the blanket, got down on bended knee:

"Child, now is not the time to flee!
We cannot pretend to understand,
but instead will remain hand in hand.

Overwhelming is the pain.
By hiding, we have nothing to gain.
With loved ones by our side, we have the opportunity to overcome.
Let us resolve never to succumb!"

Then Mom knelt on the ground.
With tears, her cheeks were drowned.

She held my hand.
The heartache she could not stand.

Her expression said it all:
"I have a confession:
My grief is overbearing.
My heart feels like it is tearing.
But, with determination
and strong captivation,
this illness may take flight.
Promise me that you will always choose to STAND and FIGHT!"

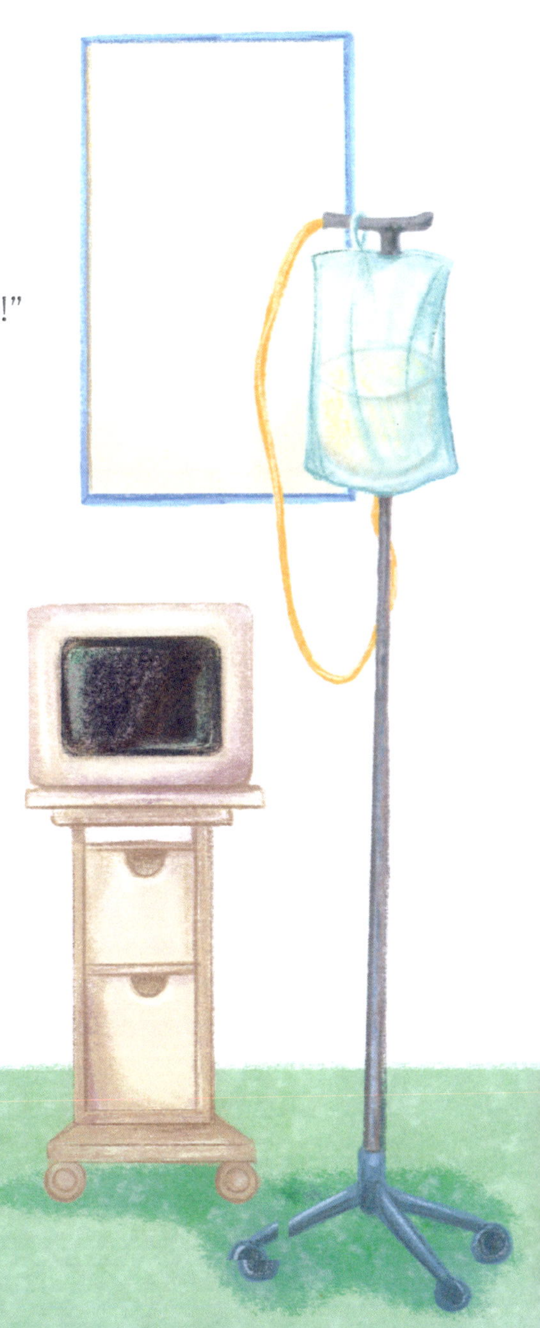

The narrative in my head I dreaded,
and so off to sleep I headed.

While I was dreaming,
I heard a voice decreeing,
"Good afternoon. You have entered the Valley of Indecision.
The territory is uncharted;
the passageway is parted."

In front of me was quite a sight.
Straddling the fence, not making any logical sense,
sat the overly dismal Giant of Uncertainty.

He appeared to have been there for quite some time:
confused and unmoved, unkempt in all his ways,
his clothing tattered, his appearance battered,
double-minded and skittish,  and extraordinarily biggish.

His storyline scattered as he continued his chatter:

"Which passage will you choose?
Either direction may leave a bruise.

Be assured, each way is daunting.
Around every bend, fear will be chomping.

Most roads traveled will cause you to
challenge yourself, brand yourself, find yourself,
and most definitely inconvenience yourself."

As I looked off in one direction,
the wet and shady crossing led
to the Marsh of Melancholy.
The sun did not appear to shine;
clouds hung heavily over the tree line.

The wind whistled a disheartening tune,
ushering in a feeling of intense gloom.

The marsh was full of pensive sadness.
It was voiceless, noiseless, and entirely joyless.

I knew this was not a place for me.

Off in the other direction stood the Triumphant Tower,
by way of the Twisted Mountain Trail–
an overly risky terrain one should not dare to travail.
A glance at the towering size and I began to bewail.

The Giant of Uncertainty continued his babble,
assuring me that my efforts would fail
and that I would become increasingly frail.

*What a woeful plight!*

Suddenly, off in the distance, I caught sight of a river,
drawn by its shimmer.

At the edge of the water,
I knelt and saw my reflection.
I knew instantly of the giant's deception.

I did not appear as the child in a hospital gown, trodden down.
I appeared polished and poised, dressed for protection:

Upon my head was a hat stamped CAPTIVATE.
Instantly, I knew all thoughts would require careful inspection
and frequent correction to head in the right direction. *(2Cor10:5)*

A belt of TRUTH was cinched around my midsection,
reminding me that circumstances are not one's self-definition,
allowing me to withstand the dangerous demands of the trail.
*(Eph 6 10-17, John 14:6)*

PEACE to guard my heart and mind for overcoming any mishap
was stitched upon my bootstrap, allowing me to face whatever
came my way, firm-footed and stable. *(Eph 6:13-18)*

Three polished stones were positioned
underneath the ripples of my reflection. *(Ex 28:21)*

GRATITUDE was etched into a carnelian stone, which reminded me how to cope
and that I should not dare to mope, but instead remain of good hope.
In all things, I must give thanks with a grateful heart. *(1Thes 5:18)*

COURAGE was carved into a stone of jasper,
which was to be continuously sought after.
I must persevere and be brave. *(Deut 31.8)*

LOVE was chiseled into an emerald stone,
which should be held on to throughout the unknowns.
I must remember that love bears all things,
hopes all things, and endures all things. *(1Cor 13:7)*

Nothing was impossible as long as I believed all things were possible.
I contemplated what I was capable of if only I tried. *(Mark 9:23)*

LOVE
COURAGE
GRATITUDE

The stones cried out victory.
Hope broke free as I picked each one up, believing they were placed there just for me.

 I could not remain double-minded or undecided in the Valley of Indecision,
so with a new self-vision, I made my decision. *(James 1:5-8)*

As I wandered the path, things did not seem all that wrong.
The sun shone brightly overhead while birds chirped a lovely song.

Up I went, very hurriedly at first, then more sluggardly,
and after a while, I trudged even more slowly.
My weary legs were barely able to carry me.

The winding path was endless. I was left breathless.
Drowsy and dull, I appeared no closer to the top than before.
Completely exhausted, I collapsed to the trail floor.

Triumphant
Tower

When suddenly, a broad-tailed creature, all crusty and bumpy,
snarly and sour, scurried in front of me just off to the side;
terrified, I wanted to hide!
He cut me off from advancing the trail; my situation became increasingly grim.
He had the most unpleasant eyes, a nauseating grin full of the most dreadfully wicked
teeth, and the most offensively foul odor oozing from the trail of slime he left behind.

Disturbing thoughts began to run through my mind.

When asked who he was, he gave a most crippling description
and called himself the Giant of Affliction.

"You thought you could sneak by," he shrieked,
"you are too weak to climb this peak.
You do not belong and may not continue along."

As he told me of all my shortcomings, my heart began
drumming faster and deeper inside my chest.

Feeling beaten down, I fearfully began to turn around,
but instead, I resolved quickly to stand firm and hold my ground.
Despite tribulation, I must keep sight of my destination.
Remembering my reflection, I fastened myself to the truth, rejecting all opposition,
and gained a peaceful position.

The Giant of Affliction came to disturb and distress; nonetheless, I came dressed in protection and purposed to prevail. *(1Sam 17:45)*

*I had the power to choose!*

Reaching inside my pocket, I pulled out the carnelian stone that reminded me of GRATITUDE; with that, I changed my attitude and released the most joyous tune.

My decree went forth and wide, and now it was no longer I who wanted to hide!
*(Job 22:28, Matthew 16:19)*

The song amplified off the mountain peaks,
creating a surprise attack,
causing the Giant of Affliction to shrink back.
Concealing his nauseating grin, his wicked teeth
could no longer mangle the truth.

I had evaded his trap with my voice and the wisdom
in the carnelian stone, belt, and bootstrap.

Renewed in hope, I continued to travail
the turns of the trail and endure the increasingly long climb.
I scaled one crest, only to discover another,
and beyond that, yet another and another.

Clinging to the jagged rocks and disappearing
behind the mountain peaks, the sun went down.
Darkness loomed all around.
Lurking shadows caused my heart to pound.

The higher I climbed, the darker it became.
My strength and courage no longer felt the same.

Out of the blackness, a hideous cackling laugh and
heckling words were heard: "What do we have here?"
snickered a wide-mouthed, curled-lip, long-nosed,
bulging-eyed giant called Scoff.

And with that, hordes of his allies filled the skies.
They came from all sides, out of every crevice and crack.
They were round-bodied, long-winged, greasy-feathered, and soiled.
Swooping down dangerously close, they taunted
and teased while snapping their dangerously sharp beaks.
Trying hard not to be dismayed and afraid, I clung to a mountain peak.

The more cowardly I became, the more empowered they became.

Eventually, after a deep breath, I began to jump from jagged rock to jagged rock,
hurriedly along the ledges, narrowly escaping into a cave called Cry Craven.

Short-tempered and testy, Scoff and his sneering horde
swarmed outside with their penetrating eyes glaring inside.

Slumping against the sheer stone wall, I cried.

Not knowing what to do, but knowing I could not remain full of fear inside the cave,
I dried my tears and tried to be brave.

The Giant of Scoff came to heckle and harass; nonetheless, I came dressed in protection
and purposed to prevail.

*I had the power to choose!*

I grasped the stones and pulled out the jasper, remembering COURAGE was a choice and
must be sought after. I was made to be brave and come out of the cave! *(Joshua 1:9)*

With faith the size of a mustard seed,
I took heed and hurled the jasper stone as a distraction.
Scoff turned his attention. Immediately,
he and his horde went off in seven other directions.
*(Matthew 17:20, Duet 28:7)*

Gingerly, I crept out of the cave,
cautiously at first, then more confidently.
After a while, I climbed even more courageously.
My strengthened legs were able to carry me.

The path no longer danced so dizzily into the sky.
Instead, my courage had caused the path to level;
negative thoughts, I was able to wrestle.

I was not full of fear but of power
and a sound mind. *(2Tim 1:7)*
The closer to the
summit I climbed,
the further the giants
were left behind.

The Giants of Uncertainty, Affliction, and Scoff had come against me; nonetheless, I came dressed in protection and purposed to prevail.

*I had the power to choose!*

In haste, I increased my pace and embraced the remaining turns of the trail, ascending to the highest peak with hinds' feet. *(2Sam 22:33-37)*

At the dawn of a new day, I had made my way
and passed through the gateway to the Triumphant Tower. *(Psalms 100:4)*

I took hold of the emerald stone, realizing it was LOVE that had hidden me in the cleft and held me in the stairway of the sky. Setting my feet on high places, I did not stumble; I overcame all my troubles.

I was not forsaken. *(Isaiah 41:10)* My hope was not taken.
I endured and believed I could.
I had travailed just as my reflection and the stones suggested I should.

Standing at the mountaintop, I took a victory stance and began to dance,
roaring with laughter for all I had sought after.

....With the sunbeams trickling across my bed,
I awoke from the dream believing that GRATITUDE, COURAGE, and LOVE
had branded me for the challenges ahead.

 My circumstances were unable to define me; with all of my might,
I knew I had the power to choose to STAND and FIGHT!

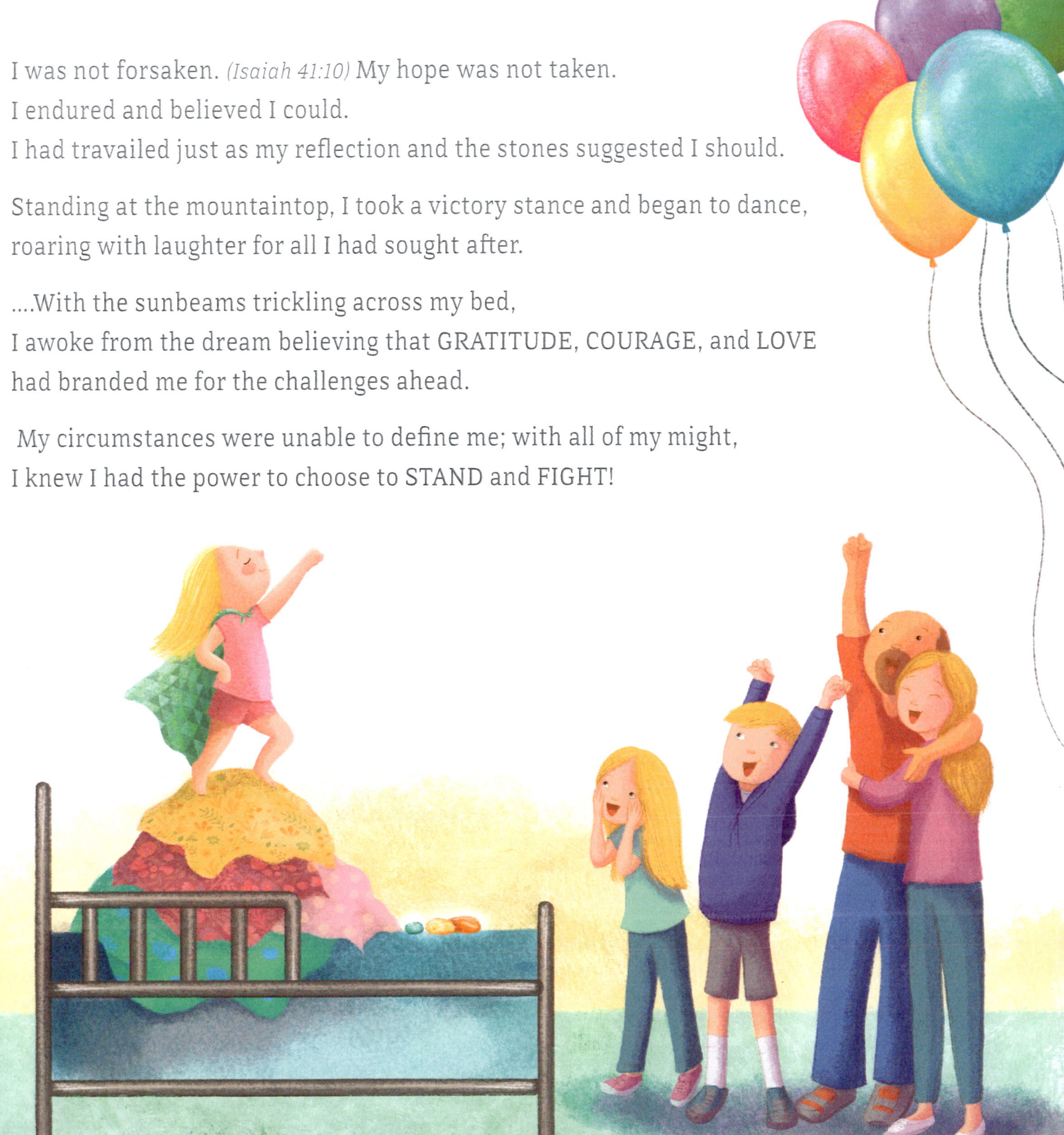

9 798218 565695